Phonics Art Projects

Fun with Phonics Through Art Grades 1–3

Marilyn Burch

Fearon Teacher Aids
23740 Hawthorne Boulevard
Torrance, CA 90505-5927
A Division of
Frank Schaffer Publications, Inc.

A Division of Frank Schaffer Publications, Inc.

ISBN–0–8224–5541–2

Printed in the United States of America
1.987654321

Table of Contents

To the Teacher

Phonics Art Projects is a teacher resource book that includes reproducible patterns and clear directions for student art projects. This delightful combination of basic skills practice and art lessons will charm students while reinforcing knowledge of basic letter-sound correspondence.

Each lesson includes

- an illustration of what the finished project might look like (allowing for individual creativity)

- a word list to be used with the lesson, at the teacher's discretion

- a list of all necessary materials

- step-by-step directions

- patterns when necessary

The finished projects may be displayed in the classroom or taken home proudly by the students. These enjoyable art projects will coordinate well with any phonics program.

A Bookmark for Big Books

b bookmark

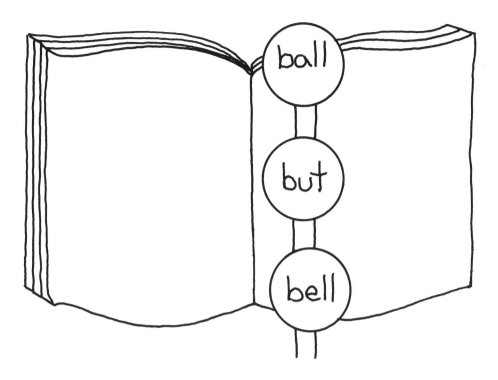

Word List

bag

back

bus

bed

ball

baby

but

big

box

bell

belt

bat

bird

body

bad

bake

Materials

Construction paper

Yarn, 12″ long (different colors)

Glue

Scissors

Crayons

Pattern

Directions

Have each child:

1. Cut 4 or 6 circles, 2″ in diameter (see pattern), from construction paper.

2. Print words starting with *b* on the circles.

3. Glue pairs of circles together, with the yarn pressed between them, so the words are on the outside. Use several strands of yarn for extra strength.

4. Use it as a bookmark.

Construct a C-Car

c car

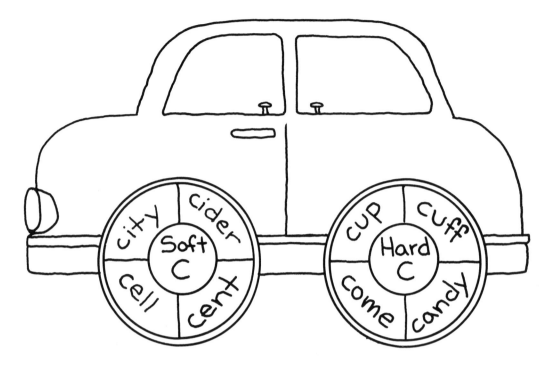

Word List

hard c

cap

call

candy

come

cane

coat

cup

cuff

soft c

city

center

cymbal

cent

cell

cereal

cement

cider

Materials

Construction paper

Scissors

Paper fasteners

Crayons

Directions

Have each child:

1. Use the pattern on the next page to cut a car from construction paper.

2. Cut out 2 tires, using the pattern.

3. Draw a hubcap on each tire. Print *soft c* on one hubcap and *hard c* on the other.

4. Section off the tires as shown. Print words with soft *c* on the tire that says *soft c.* Print words with hard *c* on the tire that says *hard c.*

5. Use paper fasteners to attach the tires to the tires on the car. Watch the tires move!

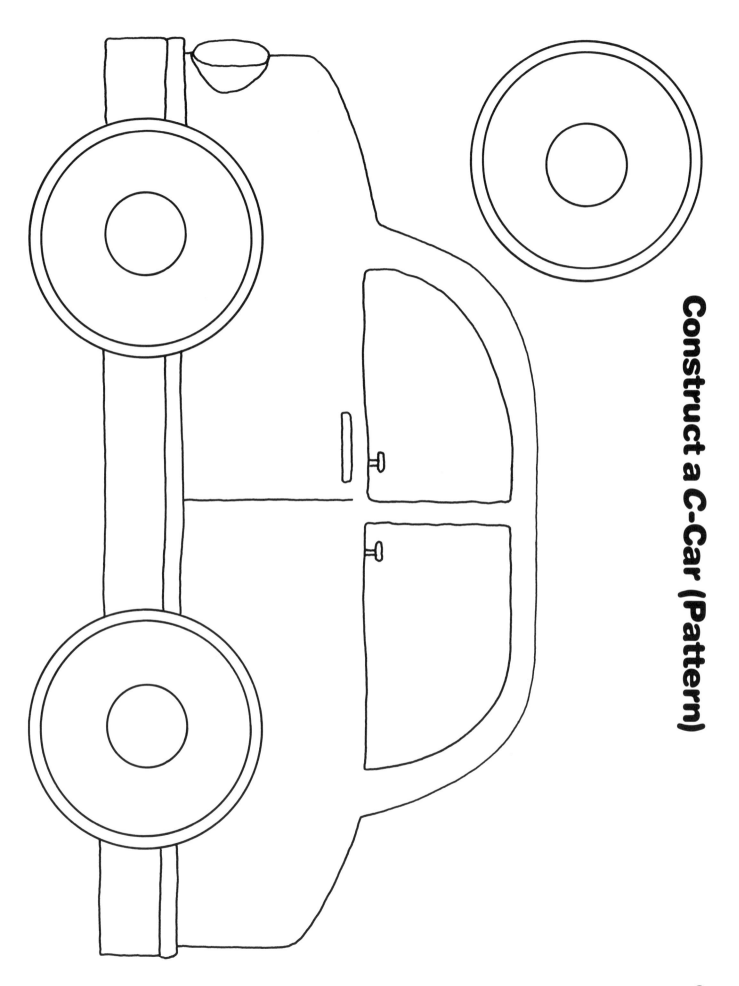

Construct a C-Car (Pattern)

3

Design a Stand-Up Dog

d   dog

Word List

did

dad

doll

day

down

do

dam

dot

door

duck

desk

dog

dab

dance

dim

deer

Materials

Tagboard, 6″ × 9″

Scissors

Glue

Crayons

Pencils

Yarn

Directions

Have each child:

1. Cut out the pattern on the next page and glue it to the tagboard.
2. Snip yarn into little pieces, about ½″ long.
3. Put dabs of glue onto the pattern within the outline of the dog. Glue the yarn to the dog so it looks like fur.
4. Use crayons to print words beginning with *d* around the dog.
5. Fold the tagboard along the dotted line; stand the dog up.

Design a Stand-Up Dog (Pattern)

Fold on dotted line.

Fine, Finny Fish

f fish

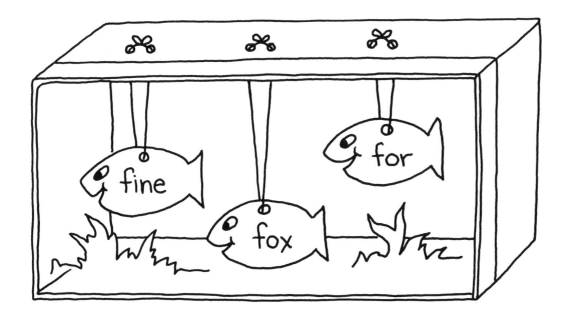

Word List

find

for

funny

four

fine

fin

fox

fish

fast

first

five

found

fall

far

full

fan

Materials

Shoe boxes

Construction paper (blue, brown, orange, and yellow)

Crayons

Scissors

String

Glue

Hole punch

Plastic wrap

Tape

Directions

Have each child:

1. Lay a shoe box on its side lengthwise.

2. On the inside, cover the sides and top with blue construction paper. Cover the inside bottom with brown construction paper. Glue the paper in place.

3. Cut fish shapes out of orange and yellow construction paper.

4. Print words beginning with *f* on the fish.

5. Punch a hole in the top of each fish. In the top of the box, punch 2 holes for each fish.

6. Insert string through the hole in the top of the fish; hang the fish inside the box, tying the string on the outside of the box.

7. Place plastic wrap over the front of the "aquarium box" and tape it to the sides.

A Good, Gentle Goose

g goose

Word List

hard g

go

good

get

gave

goes

girl

gate

gift

game

goat

soft g

ginger

gem

giant

giraffe

gym

germ

gypsy

genie

gentle

general

Materials

Scissors

Glue

Crayons

Construction paper

Directions

Have each child:

1. Cut out the goose, using the pattern on the next page. Cut along the dotted lines on the legs.

2. Cut out the strips on the next page. Fold each one in half widthwise. Open up and glue the ends of the strips together to make a stand. Set the stand aside.

3. Tear construction paper into pieces. Print soft *g* words on half the pieces and hard *g* words on the other half.

4. Glue soft *g* pieces on one side of the goose and hard *g* pieces on the other to give the goose a mosaic look.

5. Slip the stand through both legs as shown.

A Good, Gentle Goose (Pattern)

Have a Heart

h hearts

Word List

hit

he

help

has

here

hand

have

had

hen

hat

hip

her

hill

him

hem

his

hook

heel

ham

hair

Materials

Construction paper 12″ × 18″

   (red and pink)

Crayons

Scissors

Glue

Figure 1

Directions

Have each child:

1. Cut hearts out of red construction paper.

2. On the hearts, print words that begin with *h*.

3. Cut strips of red paper. Fold each one 4 times; glue the ends together to form a little box (see Figure 1).

4. Glue a box to the back of each heart and then to the pink paper. Watch the hearts nod when they are jiggled a little bit.

Jolly Jack-o'-Lantern

j jack-o'-lantern

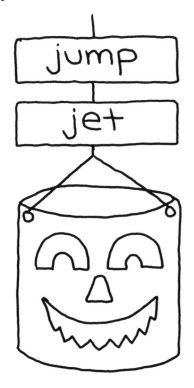

Materials

Construction paper, 9″ × 12″

String

Cards, 1½″ × 3″

Scissors

Glue

Crayon or pencil

Hole punch

Directions

Have each child:

1. Place the construction paper horizontally on a table and draw a jack-o'-lantern face in the middle third of it.

2. Cut out the eyes, nose, and mouth.

3. Roll the paper into a cylinder and glue the edges together.

4. When the glue is dry, punch 2 small holes opposite each other in the top of the lantern.

5. Tie string from one hole to the other. Tie a string to the middle of the first string and hang the lantern.

6. Print words beginning with *j* on the cards and glue them onto the string as shown.

Make a Keepsake Box

k keepsake box

Word List

key

keep

kick

kettle

kitty

kiss

kite

kid

kind

king

kit

kept

Materials

Box with a lid

Wallpaper or wrapping paper

Bits of lace, shells, buttons,
    pasta, etc.

Scissors

Glue

Crayons

Construction paper

Directions

Have each child:

1. Cover the box and its lid (separately) with wallpaper or wrapping paper.

2. Decorate the box with lace, buttons, shells, or the like.

3. Print the word *Keepsakes* on a piece of construction paper and glue it onto the lid.

4. From construction paper, cut out different shapes. Print words beginning with *k* on the shapes; put them into the box.

A Lovely Lid

l lid picture

Word List

let

ladder

little

live

left

log

lady

leaf

lame

look

lake

leak

lamb

lamp

land

letter

lap

leg

lock

lion

Materials

Box lid

Old greeting cards or magazines

Plastic wrap

Glue

Tagboard

Tape

Scissors

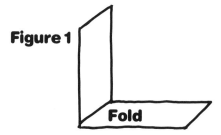

Figure 1

Fold

Directions

Have each child:

1. Look through old greeting cards or magazines and cut out pictures of things whose names start with *l*.

2. Cut strips from tagboard and fold them in half (see Figure 1).

3. Glue one half of a strip to the back of each cutout, keeping the fold at the bottom.

4. Glue the bottom half of the folded strip to the inside bottom edge of the box lid so that the cutouts can stand.

5. After finishing the scene in the box lid, put plastic wrap over the front of the lid and tape it to the sides.

A Merry Moon

m moon mobile

Word List

make

man

me

moon

my

mop

must

milk

may

made

mouse

many

much

most

mitt

mad

mail

maid

Materials

Construction paper

White thread

Crayons

Scissors

Hole punch

Directions

Have each child:

1. Use the patterns on the next page to cut out the moon and stars from construction paper. Draw a face on the moon.

2. Print words beginning with *m* on the stars. Print the word *moon* on the moon.

3. Punch holes in the bottom edge of the moon and tie thread to these holes.

4. Punch holes in the tops of the stars. Attach the stars to the thread hanging from the moon.

5. Punch a hole in the top middle of the moon. Tie thread through the hole and hang the moon up.

A Merry Moon (Pattern)

A Nice, New Necklace

n necklace

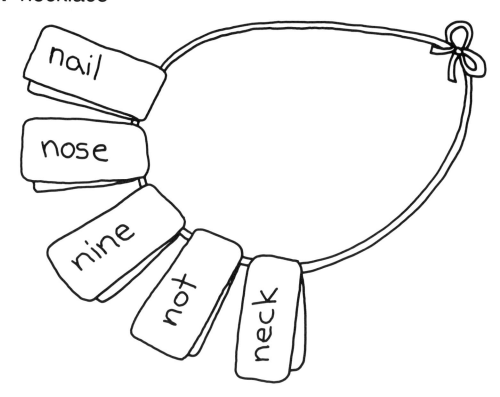

Word List

not

nest

news

no

now

nut

nail

nag

nose

nab

name

nap

new

neat

nick

nine

neck

noodle

nurse

north

Materials

Construction paper strips,
   1½″ × 6″
Yarn, 24″ long
Glue
Pencils

Directions

Have each child:

1. Fold the construction paper strips in half.
2. Print words beginning with *n* on both sides of the strips.
3. Slip the folded strips over the yarn. Glue the ends of the strips together.
4. Tie the ends of the yarn together to form a necklace.

A Pot to Put Things In

p pot

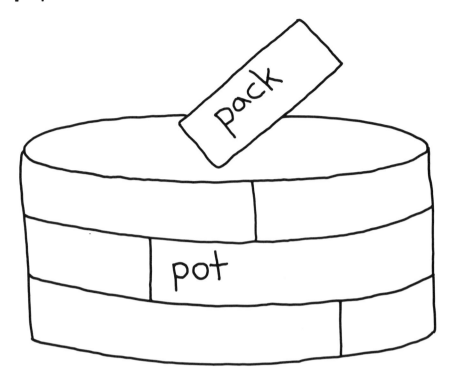

Materials

Plastic container
Ribbon or fabric cut in strips
Cards, 1½" × 3"
Crayons
Glue
Scissors

Directions

Have each child:

1. Glue strips of ribbon or fabric around the plastic container.
2. Print words beginning with *p* on cards.
3. Place the cards in the pot.

Word List
pie
pay
pin
paint
pick
pair
pencil
pull
pack
party
picture
pad
pail
pet
paw
pig
page
pan
pain
pipe

A Quart of Quarters

q quarter bank

Word List

quick

quail

quake

quart

queen

quarter

quilt

quiet

question

quiz

Materials

Baking powder or nut can with
   plastic lid (not a can with sharp
   edges)
Construction paper
Scissors
Glue or tape
Pencils or crayons

Directions

Have each child:

1. Print the word *quarters* on construction paper. Wrap the construction
paper around the can; glue or tape it onto the can.

2. In the plastic lid, cut a slit large enough to accommodate a quarter.

3. Cut out "quarters" from construction paper. Print words beginning with *q*
on the quarters.

4. Deposit the quarters into the bank after reading the words correctly.

Rings to Read

r rings

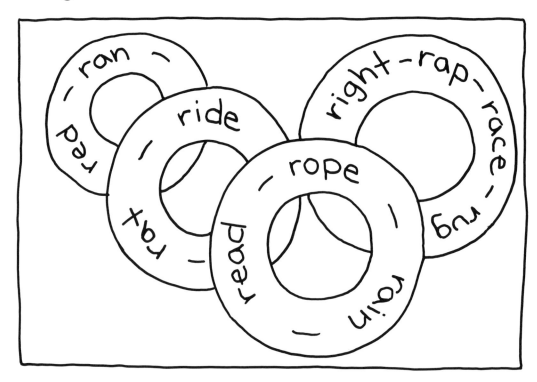

Word List

Word List

red

ran

rat

ride

rain

read

rope

right

rap

race

rack

ring

rabbit

rose

rug

roof

rail

rake

rag

rate

Materials

Construction paper, 12″ × 18″

Glue

Scissors

Crayons

Directions

Have each child:

1. Cut out rings from construction paper, using the patterns on the next page.
2. Print words that begin with *r* around the rings. Put dashes between the words to separate them.
3. Glue the rings to construction paper, making a ring design.

Rings to Read (Pattern)

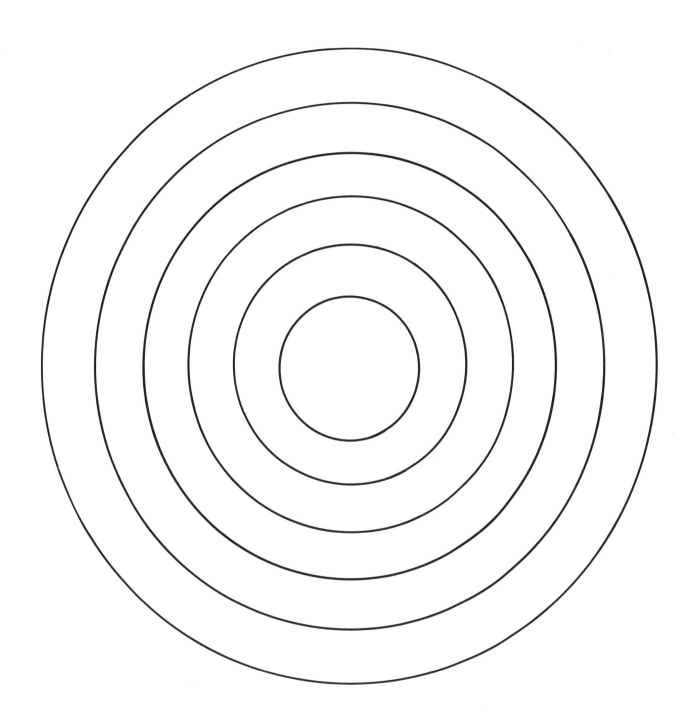

19

That's Some Sun!

s sun

Word List

sit

said

sun

see

saw

sock

so

say

sing

six

side

soap

soon

seven

some

sink

seed

sail

Materials

Construction paper, 12″ × 18″
   (blue and yellow)

Crayons

Scissors

Glue

Directions

Have each child:

1. Cut out a large circle from yellow construction paper; glue it onto the blue paper.

2. Draw a face on the circle and print the word *sun* on it.

3. Cut strips from the yellow paper. On the strips, print words that start with *s.* Glue the strips around the sun to look like rays.

A Tall and Tidy Tepee

t tepee

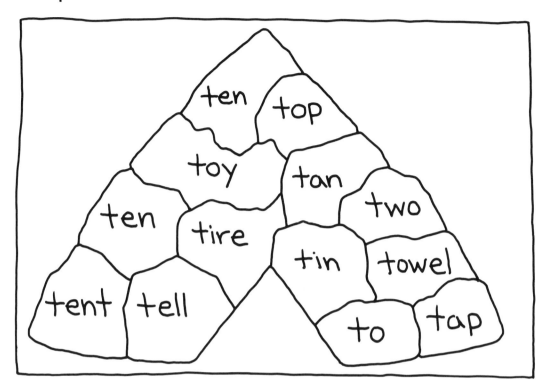

Word List

table

to

ten

two

tell

take

towel

tie

time

tall

tire

top

too

tin

ton

toy

tent

tar

tulip

tip

Materials

Construction paper (various colors)

Pencils

Glue

Directions

Have each child:

1. From construction paper, tear pieces large enough to print words on.
2. Print words beginning with *t* on the pieces.
3. Glue the pieces onto another piece of construction paper to form a tepee.

Very Good Vegetables

v vegetables

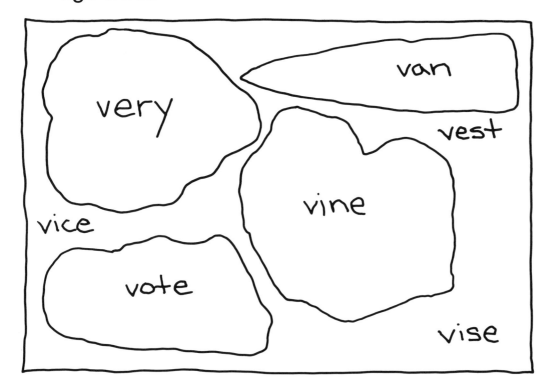

Word List

vest

very

vase

violin

vale

vice

villa

visit

vine

valentine

vain

van

vote

vise

Materials

Vegetables (potatoes, carrots,
    cauliflower, broccoli, celery), cut
    to show different shapes and
    textures
Tempera
Brushes
Manila paper
Crayons or pencils

Directions

Have each child:

1. Paint the surfaces of the vegetables, or dip them in the tempera.

2. Roll the painted surfaces on the Manila paper to create an abstract, colorful design.

3. When the paint dries, print words that begin with *v* on and around the painted areas.

A Wonderful, Well-Made Wagon

w wagon

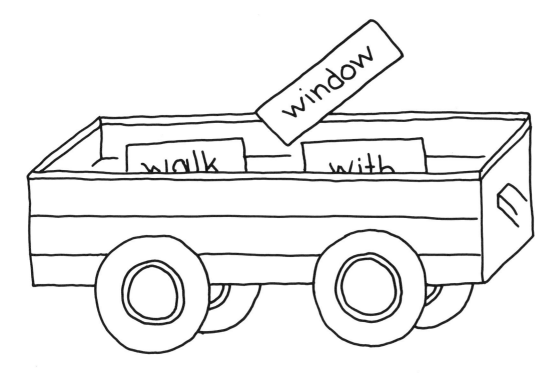

Word List

wagon

we

want

was

watch

well

web

went

wing

window

walk

will

wish

with

wash

work

wall

wind

Materials

Large matchbox

Tagboard

Construction paper

Glue

Pencils or crayons

Scissors

Directions

Have each child:

1. Cut out circles from the tagboard; glue the circles onto the matchbox for wheels.

2. Cut pieces of tagboard or construction paper to fit in the matchbox.

3. Print words that begin with *w* on the pieces of tagboard or construction paper; place them in the wagon.

Make an Ax

x ax

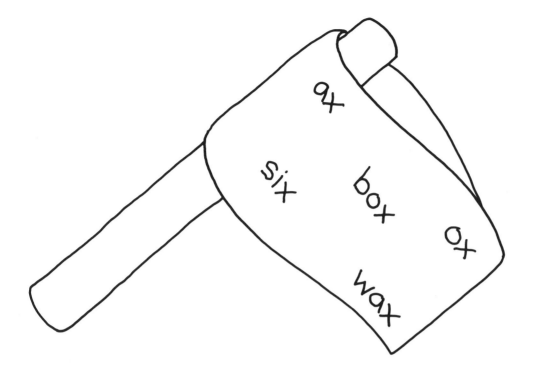

Word List

ax

ox

six

wax

fox

lax

box

Materials

Cardboard roll

Construction paper strips, 4″ × 12″

Glue

Crayons or pencils

Directions

Have each child:

1. On a strip of construction paper, print words that have the *x* sound.
2. Fold the strip over one end of the cardboard roll; glue it to the roll.
3. Glue the ends of the strip together.

A Yarn Design on Yellow

y yarn

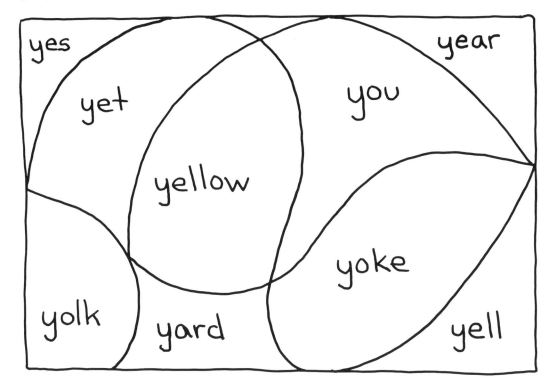

Word List

yes

you

yellow

yard

year

yoke

your

yolk

yarn

yell

yet

yule

Materials

Yellow construction paper

Yarn

Glue

Black crayon

Directions

Have each child:

1. Glue yarn on yellow construction paper in a design.
2. Print words that begin with *y* inside the shapes formed by the yarn.

A Zoo for You

Z ZOO

Materials

Box lid

Animal pictures cut from
  magazines

Construction paper

Scissors

Glue

Pencils or crayons

Directions

Have each child:

1. Cover the box lid with construction paper.

2. Print words that start with *z* around the lid.

3. Glue animal pictures onto construction paper for reinforcement. Cut the pictures out. Glue a tab on the back of each picture so it will stand up.

4. Stand the animals up in the lid. Cut out strips of paper and paste them over the front of the cage for bars.

Make a Vase

ā vase

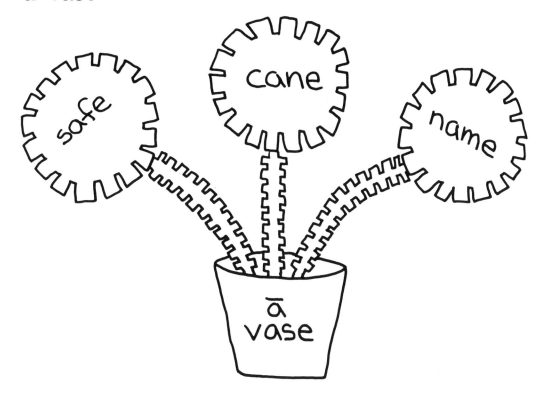

Materials

Construction paper, 9″ × 12″

Construction paper circles, 2½″ in diameter

Green construction paper stems, 6″ × ¾″

Crayons

Construction paper rectangles, 9″ × 4″ (cut 9″ × 12″ paper into thirds)

Scissors

Glue

Ruler

Directions

Have each child:

1. Print long *a* words on the construction paper circles.

2. Cut an even number of slits (each about ½″ deep) around the edges of the circles; fold every other slit in.

3. Cut slits along both sides of the stems; bend alternate cuts forward.

4. Glue the stems and blossoms on a 9″ × 12″ vertical piece of construction paper.

5. Print ā vase in the center of the rectangle, as shown.

6. Fold back the short sides of the rectangle at an angle; glue them over the bottom part of the stems, forming a vase.

A Tree to See

ē ēa ēē tree

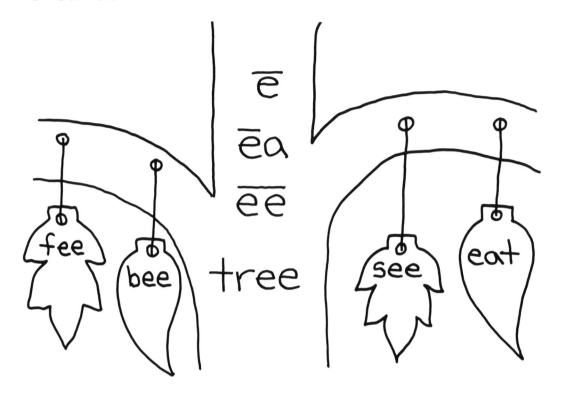

Materials

Construction paper, 9″ × 12″
   (brown, red, yellow, green,
   and orange)
Thread

Crayons
Hole punch
Scissors

Directions

Have each child:

1. Cut out the tree trunk from brown construction paper, using the pattern on the next page.

2. Cut out 4 leaves from red, yellow, green, and orange construction paper, using the patterns on the next page.

3. Punch holes as indicated on the patterns.

4. Print long *e* words on both sides of the leaves. Print *ē, ēa, ēē,* and the word *tree* on both sides of the tree trunk.

5. Hang the leaves on the tree by tying thread through the holes in the tops of the leaves to the holes in the branches.

6. Tie the tree to a high object, using a thread inserted through the hole in the top of the tree trunk.

<table>
<tr><td>Word List</td></tr>
<tr><td>jeep</td></tr>
<tr><td>keep</td></tr>
<tr><td>beef</td></tr>
<tr><td>deep</td></tr>
<tr><td>feet</td></tr>
<tr><td>sneeze</td></tr>
<tr><td>sheep</td></tr>
<tr><td>weep</td></tr>
<tr><td>street</td></tr>
<tr><td>sleeve</td></tr>
<tr><td>geese</td></tr>
<tr><td>neat</td></tr>
<tr><td>eat</td></tr>
<tr><td>heap</td></tr>
<tr><td>bean</td></tr>
<tr><td>meat</td></tr>
<tr><td>beads</td></tr>
<tr><td>peak</td></tr>
<tr><td>lead</td></tr>
<tr><td>mean</td></tr>
<tr><td>leap</td></tr>
<tr><td>dream</td></tr>
</table>

A Tree to See (Pattern)

29

I Like Kites

ī kites

five fine nine

like bike kite

Materials

Construction paper, 9″ × 12″

Yarn

Crayons

Scissors

Glue

Figure 1

Cut.

Glue to paper.

Glue to back of kite.

Directions

Have each child:

1. Cut out 2 kite shapes from construction paper.

2. Print long *i* words on the kites.

3. Cut out 2 circles, 2″ in diameter. Keep cutting around inside the circle to make a spring, as shown in Figure 1.

4. Glue the center of the spring to the back of the kite.

5. Glue the end of the spring to a 9″ × 12″ sheet of construction paper.

6. Cut 2 pieces of yarn, 6″ long. Glue each "tail" to a kite and to the construction paper.

7. From construction paper, cut out "ties" for the tail; glue them onto the yarn.

Oh! A Cone!

ō cone

cone
tone
alone
bone

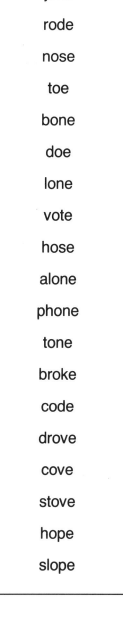

Word List

home

joke

rode

nose

toe

bone

doe

lone

vote

hose

alone

phone

tone

broke

code

drove

cove

stove

hope

slope

Materials

Construction paper (brown and
   various colors)

Tissue paper

Glue

Crayons

Scissors

Directions

Have each child:

1. Round off the top of a 6″ × 12″ strip of brown
   construction paper.

2. Fold the brown paper in 2 places, as shown, to form
   a cone.

3. Glue the cone to a 9″ × 12″ sheet of construction
   paper.

4. Print words with long *o* on the cone.

5. Glue a crumpled piece of tissue paper onto the top
   of the cone.

Ice Cubes for You

ū cube

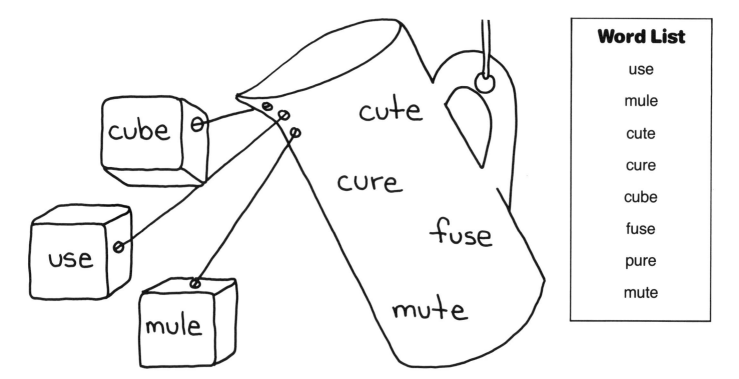

Word List

use

mule

cute

cure

cube

fuse

pure

mute

Materials

Construction paper

Thread

Glue

Crayons

Scissors

Hole punch

Directions

Have each child:

1. Draw and cut out a pitcher and 3 shapes that look like ice cubes.
2. Put long *u* words on both sides of the pitcher and the ice cubes.
3. Punch a hole into the handle and into each ice cube; punch 3 holes into the spout.
4. Cut 3 different lengths of thread; use them to tie the cubes to the pitcher at the spout.
5. Cut another, longer piece of thread; use it to tie to the handle and hang to an object.

A Zigzag Mat

ă mat

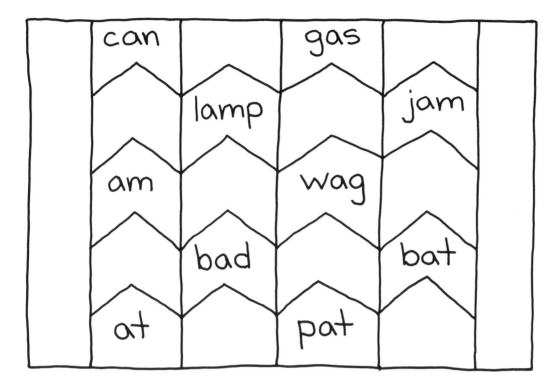

Materials

Dark and light construction paper,
   9″ × 12″
Black bulletin board paper
Bulletin board
Crayons
Ruler
Thumbtacks
Scissors

Directions

Have each child:

1. Cut a dark piece of construction paper the long way in zigzag or curved lines about 1½″ wide, leaving an uncut margin around the paper.

2. Cut a light piece of construction paper into straight strips the same width as the zigzags. Weave the strips through the darker paper; tape the edges down to the uncut margins.

3. Print short *a* words on the light areas of the mat.

4. Tack the mats to a bulletin board covered with black bulletin board paper, leaving black spaces between the mats.

The Best Belt Ever!

ĕ belt

Materials

Butcher paper or shelf paper

Scissors

Tape

Crayons

Measuring tape

Directions

Have each child:

1. Measure his or her waist.

2. On the paper, draw 2 parallel lines, 1½″ apart and about 4″ longer than the waist measurement.

3. Print short *e* words between the lines, using different colors of crayons and adding designs if desired. Leave the extra 2 inches on each side blank for overlapping, or add special decoration to the part that will go on top.

4. Cut out this decorated strip of paper.

5. Put this "belt" around the waist, overlapping the ends and using tape to secure it.

Word List

belt

web

hen

pen

men

leg

beg

fence

tent

desk

well

bell

sell

tell

fed

led

pet

jet

wet

west

Inch by Inch

ĭ inch

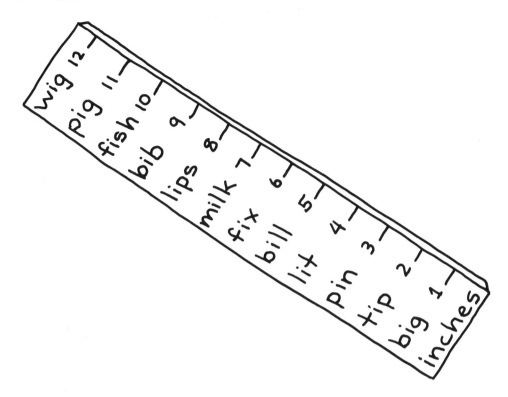

Materials

Tagboard pieces, 2″ × 12″

Ruler

Crayons

Directions

Have each child:

1. Lay a ruler alongside the length of the tagboard strip. Mark off the inches with a slash. Place the inch numbers by their slashes.

2. Print words that have short *i* on the ruler, opposite the slashes. Print the word *inches* at the bottom of the tagboard ruler.

Word List
ring
sing
wing
six
mix
fix
bill
fish
will
pig
dip
big
wig
lift
lips
milk
bib
lit
tip
pin

Gobs of Logs

ŏ log

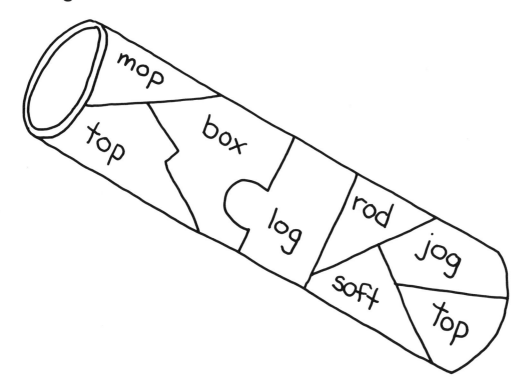

Word List

mop

top

pop

box

ox

fox

dot

got

rot

hot

soft

loft

jog

hog

bog

fond

pond

sod

rod

doll

Materials

Cardboard roll

Construction paper

Crayons

Glue

Scissors

Directions

Have each child:

1. Cut out different shapes from various colors of paper.

2. Print short *o* words on the shapes.

3. Glue the shapes onto the cardboard "log."

4. The logs can be stacked as a wood pile in the room. During reading class, students can pick any log and read the words on it.

A Funny, Little Hut

ŭ hut

Word List

rug

jug

tug

mug

bug

sun

gun

run

bun

us

cub

tub

hub

sub

cut

rut

bus

cup

gum

up

Materials

Small box

Construction paper (brown
   and black)

Glue

Crayons

Scissors

Directions

Have each child:

1. Glue brown construction paper to the outside of a small box.

2. Use crayons to draw a door and windows on the box.

3. Cut out roof "thatch" strips from black and brown paper, making a point
    at one end of each strip.

4. Print words containing short *u* on the roof strips. Glue the strips onto the
    roof, letting the pointed ends hang over the edge of the box.

5. Bend the strips to hang over the edge.

Waiting for Rain

ai rain

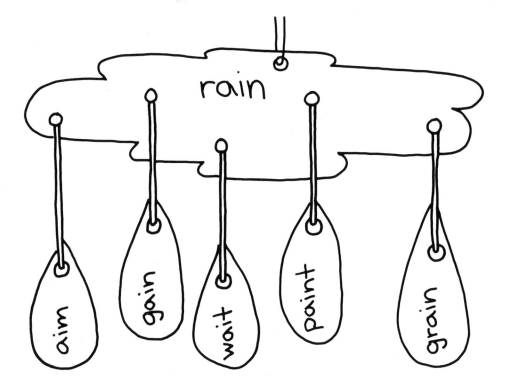

Word List

wait

main

aim

train

pain

drain

stain

gain

rain

bait

chain

paint

claim

grain

Materials

White construction paper,
  12″ × 18″
Scissors
Hole punch
Thread
Crayons

Directions

Have each child:

1. Cut out a cloud shape from white construction paper. Print the word *rain* on it.

2. Cut out 5 to 7 raindrops from the white paper. Print words with *ai* on the raindrops.

3. Punch 5 to 7 holes in the bottom of the cloud. Punch a hole in the top of each raindrop. Tie the raindrops to the bottom of the cloud with thread.

4. Punch a hole in the top of the cloud. Put thread through the hole; hang the cloud as a mobile.

A Day to Play with Clay

ay clay

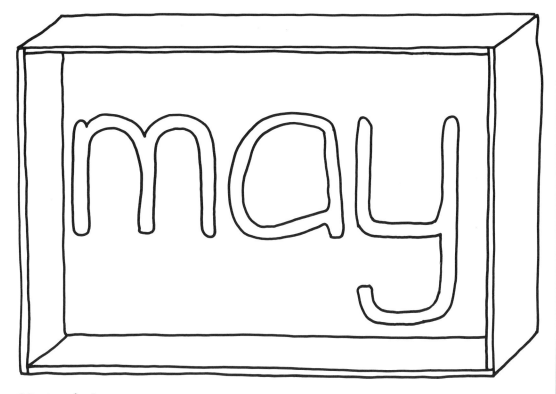

Word List

pay

gay

lay

may

bay

jay

play

ray

hay

day

way

say

stay

tray

Materials

Box lid, shallow and small
Plasticine™ clay

Directions

Have each child:

1. Roll the clay into the form of a snake.
2. Use pieces of the snake shape to form the letters of an *ay* word.
3. Press the clay to the lid. It will stay.

Floating Boats

oa boat

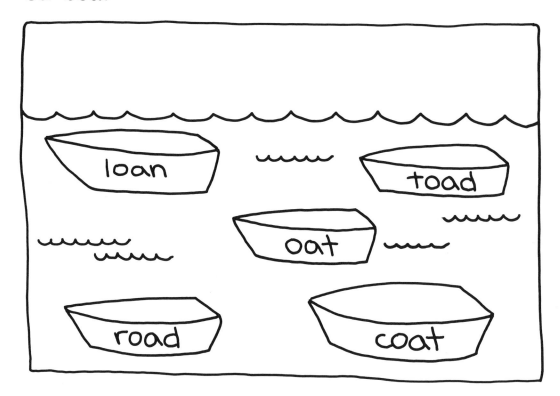

Word List
soap
coat
road
loan
load
float
goal
toad
goat
boat
moan
oat
coal
moat

Materials

Construction paper 9″ × 12″
   (different shades of the
   same color)

Scissors

Glue

Crayons

Directions

Have each child:

1. Glue a 3″ × 12″ piece of light construction paper to the top third of a darker piece, 9″ × 12″.

2. From other shades of the same color of construction paper, cut out large and small boats.

3. Print words with *oa* on the boats.

4. Glue the boats to the lower two-thirds of the background.

5. Draw wavy lines to represent water.

A Wise, Brown Owl

ow owl

Materials

Paper lunch bag

Construction paper (various colors)

Old newspapers

Scissors

Glue

Crayons

String

Directions

Have each child:

1. Cut out feathers of different colors from construction paper. Print words with *ow* on the feathers.

2. Cut out 2 feet, 2 ears, 2 eyes, and a beak.

3. Stuff a lunch bag with newspaper; tie it shut.

4. Glue the feathers, feet, ears, eyes, and beak onto the owl.

Word List

plow

how

cow

crowd

towel

bow

owl

howl

cowboy

crown

clown

gown

town

brown

down

shower

power

flower

A Wise, Brown Owl (Patterns)

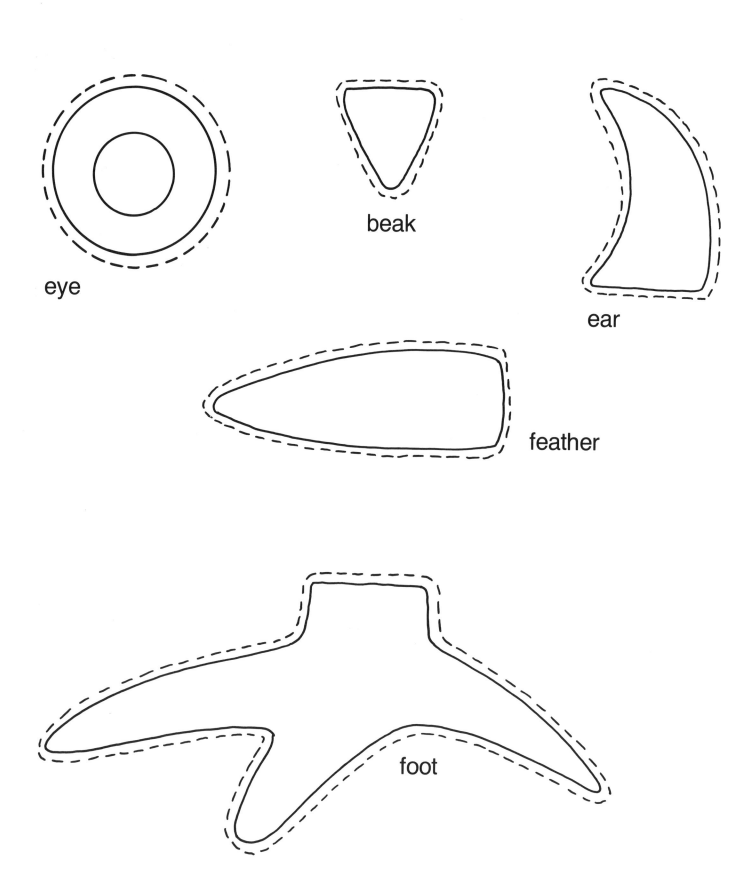

eye

beak

ear

feather

foot

Show What You Know

ōw slow

Word List

snow

bow

crow

own

know

show

grow

elbow

rainbow

snowman

bowl

low

slow

flow

mow

below

Materials

Yellow construction paper,
   9″ × 12″

Strip of cardboard, 2″ × 18″

Scissors

Black crayon

Glue

Directions

Have each child:

1. Print the word *Slow* across the top of the sheet of yellow construction paper. Below this, print *Children Crossing*.

2. Glue the strip of cardboard to the back of the yellow sign. Be sure at least 9″ of the strip is glued onto the back.

3. On the back of the sign, print words that have *ow* as in *slow.*

About the House

ou house

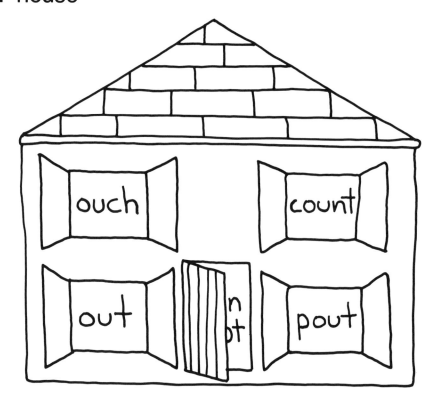

Materials

Construction paper (light and dark)

Scissors

Glue

Crayons

Directions

Have each child:

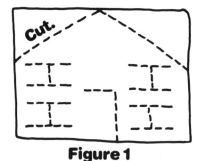

Figure 1

1. Cut a house out of dark paper. Cut the windows and door open by cutting along the dotted lines, as shown in Figure 1.

2. Glue the house onto the light-colored paper. (Be sure to avoid gluing down the windows and door.)

3. Open the door and windows; print *ou* words behind the openings.

Word List
house
mouse
ouch
couch
pouch
cloud
mouth
ground
mount
noun
pout
out
trout
stout
shout
hound
mountain
count
about
scout

Make a Coil

oi coil

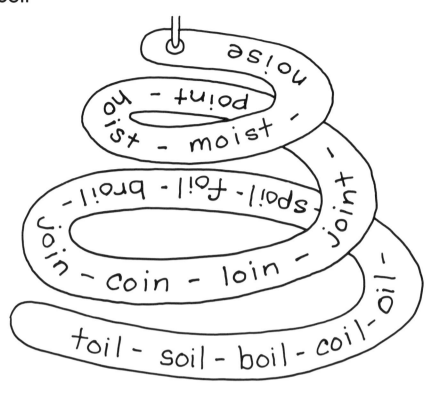

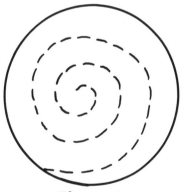

Cut along dotted lines.

Figure 1

Word List

toil

soil

boil

coil

oil

spoil

foil

broil

join

coin

loin

joint

point

hoist

moist

noise

Materials

Construction paper, 9″ square

Scissors

Hole punch

String

Black crayon

Directions

Have each child:

1. Cut out a circle, 8″ in diameter.

2. Cut this circle in a spiral, as shown in Figure 1.

3. Punch a hole in the smaller end. Put a string through the hole so that the coil can be hung.

4. Print words that contain *oi* around the coil. Put dashes between the words to separate them.

5. Hang the coil as a mobile.

Toys for Joy

oy toy

Word List

boy

toy

Roy

royal

voyage

joy

enjoy

destroy

loyal

employ

Materials

Boxes (various sizes)

Construction paper

Magazines

Glue

Scissors

Crayons

Directions

Have each child:

1. Cover a box with construction paper.
2. Cut out pictures of toys from magazines. Glue these pictures onto pieces of construction paper and put them in the box.
3. Print *oy* words on the toy box.

A Cool Moon

$\overline{oo}$ moon

Word List

boom

soothe

zoo

too

spool

stool

pool

broom

goose

drool

moo

noon

cool

tool

fool

spoon

Materials

Construction paper, 9″ × 12″
  (black and white)

Scissors

Glue

White crayon or chalk

Directions

Have each child:

1. Cut out a large moon from white construction paper; glue it onto the black construction paper.

2. Draw trees, a skyline, and stars with a white crayon or chalk.

3. Print $\overline{oo}$ *moon* at the top of the paper with white crayon or chalk.

4. Print other $\overline{oo}$ words at the bottom of the scene.

Look at This Bookmark!

ŏŏ bookmark

book
good
took
look
cook

Materials

Construction paper strips, 2″ × 6″

Crayons

Scissors

Directions

Have each child:

1. Draw a bird face on the top third of one bookmark strip. Draw a V for a beak.

2. Cut along the V, being careful not to cut the beak out.

3. Print words that contain ŏŏ on the lower part of the bookmark.

4. Use the beak to mark a page by placing the beak over the page, as shown.

News Items

ew news

Words in bubble: dew new / grew blew / crew dew / stew flew / drew chew

Word List

dew

new

grew

drew

crew

brew

threw

screw

stew

blew

chew

flew

Materials

Round lid from a cereal box
Construction paper (brown,
   black, and white)
Tape
Scissors
Glue
Crayons

Directions

Have each child:

1. Cut out brown construction paper to fit the round lid. Cut out a strip of brown construction paper to fit around the rim. Glue both pieces onto the lid to cover it.

2. Cut out a cat's eyes, nose, ears, whiskers, and mouth from black construction paper. Glue them onto the lid.

3. Cut out a "bubble" from white construction paper. Print words that contain *ew* in the bubble.

4. Tape the cat's head to a sheet of brown construction paper. Glue the bubble to the paper, as shown.

Because It's Autumn

au autumn

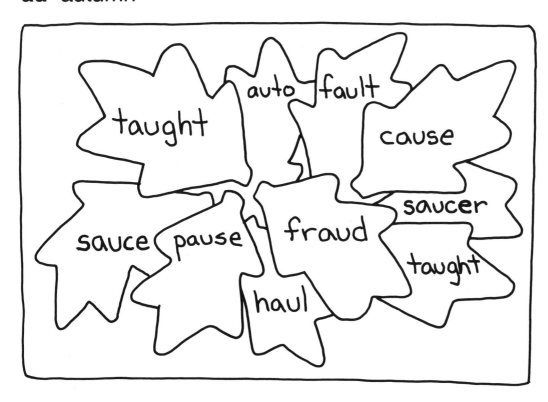

taught auto fault cause sauce pause fraud saucer haul taught

Materials

Black construction paper, 9″ × 12″

Construction paper (yellow, green,
   red, and orange)

Scissors

Glue

Crayons

Directions

Have each child:

1. Cut out leaf shapes from different colors of construction paper.

2. Print *au* words on the leaves.

3. Glue the leaves onto the black construction paper, overlapping them
   and leaving a margin of black around them.

We Saw a Saw of Straws

aw straw saw

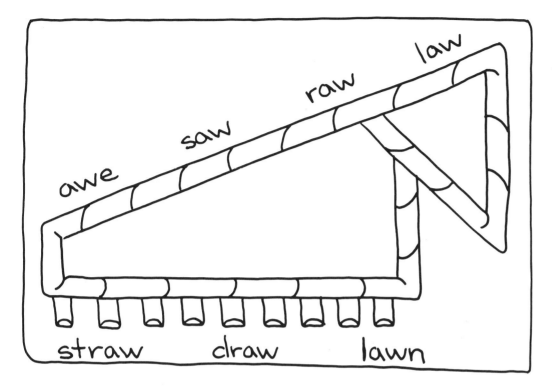

Materials

Blue construction paper

White paper straws

Glue

Scissors

Crayons

Directions

Have each child:

1. Lay white straws out on the blue construction paper in an outline of a saw, as shown.

2. Glue the straws down.

3. When the glue is dry, print *aw* words around the outside of the saw.

Word List

awe

saw

paw

raw

straw

law

draw

thaw

squawk

fawn

lawn

yawn

claw

crawl

hawk

awful

Larks in the Park

ar lark

Word List

barn

car

far

yarn

bark

dart

part

ark

hard

star

park

farm

jar

cart

arm

mark

lark

lard

Materials

Manila paper

Crayons

Hole punch

Scissors

String or thread

Directions

Have each child:

1. Cut out a bird from Manila paper, using the pattern on the next page.

2. Print the word *lark* on the bird. On the other side of the bird, print words that have *ar* in them.

3. Color the bird on both sides.

4. Punch a hole in the top of the bird, tie on a thread, and hang the bird up.

Larks in the Park (Pattern)

Deliver the Letters

er letters

Materials

Construction paper, 12″ × 18″
   and 9″ × 12″
Tape (optional)
Crayons or black felt-tip pen
Glue

Directions

Have each child:

1. Cut a 9″ × 12″ piece of construction paper down to 9″ × 8″.

2. Print the word *letters* across the center of this piece.

3. Roll up the paper, keeping the word *letters* on the outside. Glue the ends together, and glue or tape it onto the 12″ × 18″ piece of construction paper to make a mailbox.

4. Roll the remaining 9″ × 4″ piece of construction paper and glue the ends together. Then glue this piece to the 12″ × 18″ piece to make the mailbox post.

5. Cut out rectangle shapes ("envelopes") from various colors of construction paper. On these, print words that have *er* in them. Glue the "letters" to the construction paper, as shown.

Word List

fern
hammer
jerk
perch
clerk
thunder
mother
pepper
letter
ruler
verse
her
feather
father
person
under

Whirls, Twirls, and Circles

ir circle

Materials
Manila paper
Crayons
Paint (optional)

Directions
Have each child:

1. Draw or paint circles and half circles on the Manila paper. Make designs inside the circles, as desired.
2. Print *ir* words around the circles.

Word List

whirl

shirt

skirt

firm

circus

birch

chirp

thirsty

stir

twirl

irk

circle

birthday

sir

dirt

fir

More Corn for You?

or corn

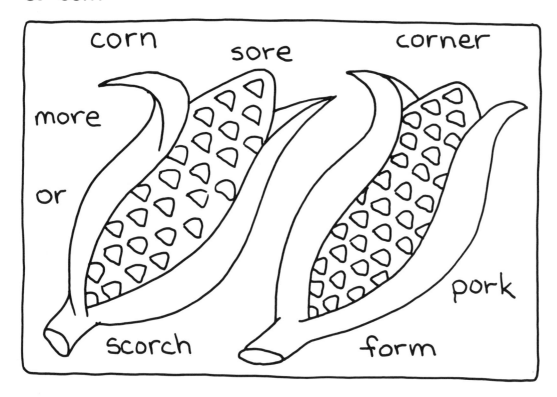

Materials

Construction paper, 9″ × 12″
   (orange, yellow, and green)
Glue
Black crayon or felt-tip pen
Scissors

Directions

Have each child:

1. Draw ears of corn with husks on the orange paper.
2. Tear or cut out small pieces of yellow construction paper.
3. Glue these pieces onto the drawing of corn.
4. Cut or tear green pieces of construction paper and glue these pieces onto the husks.
5. Print *or* words around the corn.

Word List

corn

storm

corner

more

store

horn

cork

form

sore

story

short

pork

scorch

born

fork

port

Don't Hurt the Turtle!

ur turtle

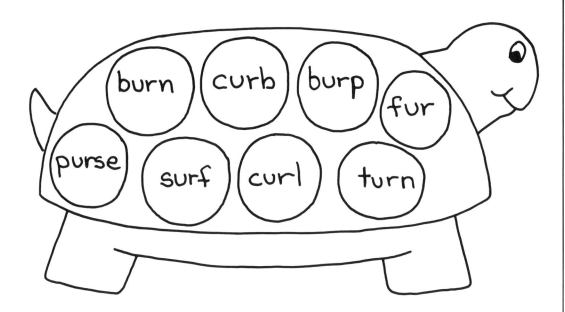

Word List

turkey

turtle

purse

church

fur

burp

lurk

curve

curl

turn

burn

curb

curd

curt

turf

murk

surf

hurt

Materials

Tagboard, 9″ × 12″

Crayons

Scissors

Directions

Have each child:

1. Use the pattern on the next page to cut out the turtle from tagboard.
2. Draw large circles on the turtle's shell. In the circles, print words that have *ur* in them.
3. Color in the turtle's features and shell.
4. Fold down on the lines marked A.
5. Fold up on the lines marked B.
6. Stand the turtle up.

Don't Hurt the Turtle! (Pattern)

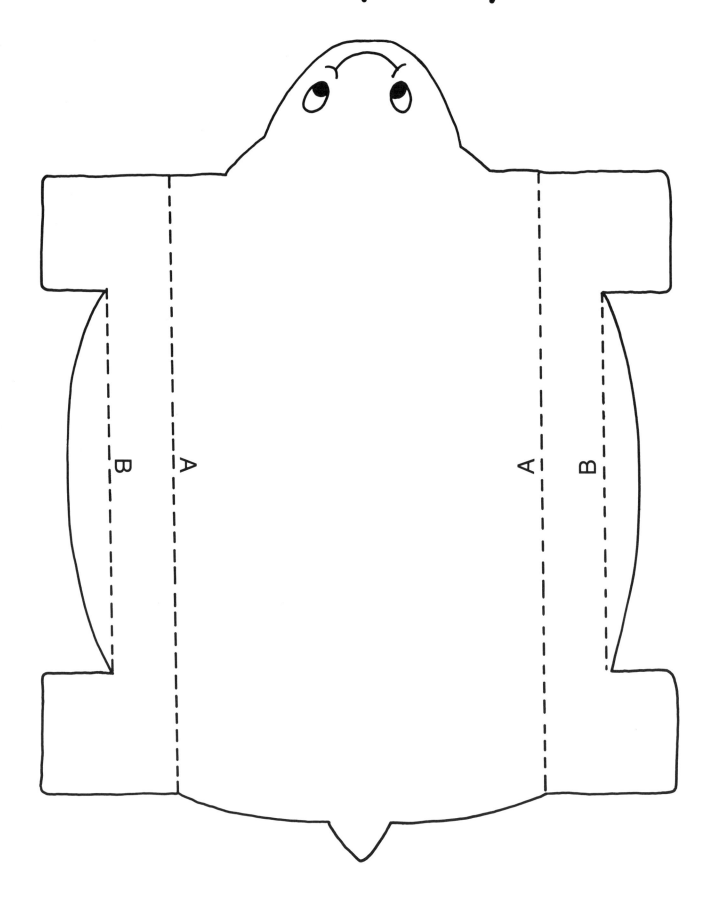

Checkers or Chess, Anyone?

ch checkerboard

A checkerboard with words on the white squares:

chew		cheer		cheat		chat
	champ		chalk		chase		chin
chain		chill		chess		check
	cheap		chap		cheese		chick
chair		cheek		chip		chant
	chance		change		choke		chilly
char		chore		charge		chop
	chart		chief		cherry		chest

Word List

- chew
- cheer
- cheat
- chat
- choke
- chalk
- chime
- chase
- chip
- chin
- chain
- chill
- chess
- check
- cheap
- change
- cheese
- child
- chick
- chop
- chair
- cheek

Materials

Red construction paper, 12″ × 18″

Black construction paper, 9″ × 12″

Ruler

Scissors

Glue

Black crayon or felt-tip pen

Directions

Have each child:

1. Draw 7 lines, 1½″ apart, across the width of a 12″ square of red construction paper. Do the same across the length, making 64 squares.

2. Draw 32 1½″ squares on a 9″ × 12″ piece of black construction paper. Cut out these squares and glue them onto the red paper, making a checkerboard. (The lower left corner should be black.)

3. Print words that begin with *ch* on the red squares. (Words can be repeated.)

4. From the remaining black and red paper, cut out 12 red circles and 12 black circles. Use the board and pieces to play checkers.

Shadow Shapes

sh shadows

Materials

Desk lamp or flashlight

Crayons

Manila paper, 9″ × 12″

Directions

1. Tape down a piece of Manila paper on each desk.

2. Shine a lamp or hold a flashlight over the piece of paper. Have each child hold one hand between the light and the paper, and trace the outline of the hand shadow.

3. Have each child then draw and color in a picture made from the hand shadow.

4. Have the children print *sh* words around their pictures.

Word List

shack

shag

she

sham

shape

shark

shave

shed

shade

shake

shall

shame

share

sharp

show

sheep